Cupcake and Noodles Go To Kenya

Angie Stubbs

Archway Publishing books may be ordered through booksellers or by contacting:

Archway Publishing
1663 Liberty Drive
Bloomington, IN 47403
www.archwaypublishing.com
1 (888) 242-5904

ISBN: 978-1-4808-6349-1 (sc)
ISBN: 978-1-4808-6350-7 (hc)
ISBN: 978-1-4808-6351-4 (e)

Print information available on the last page.

Archway Publishing rev. date: 7/16/2018

This book is dedicated to Anna and
Naomi (Cupcake and Noodles).
It is such a joy to experience
this world with you and to see
through your eyes. To my husband,
Quentin, thanks for all the love
and support. You are amazing.

Cupcake and Noodles like to travel in cars, on buses, and in planes.
They go many places, and none are the same.
They like the mountains, city and beach-wherever they can play, make friends, and eat!
This month, November, they leave with Mom, Dad and Grandma Emma
to visit a beautiful country called Kenya.
Kenya has mountains, big tall buildings, and beaches with lots of sand.
It has lions, gazelles and other creatures that roam the land.
Cupcake and Noodles are very excited, you see, for it's their first time in the capital, Nairobi.

On the first day, Cupcake rushes Mom and Dad to see the giraffes before its gets dark,
so where do they go? Nairobi National Park!
Oh, Noodles will stay at the hotel. Mom and Dad think that's best,
since Noodles and Grandma Emma need to get their rest.
At the park, Mom and Cupcake take a picture with tribesmen called Massai.
And when the men sing, they jump very high.

Big baboons, rhinos, and zebras pass them by. Colorful birds fly high in the sky!
Look at the grass! Look at the trees! Look at the lion cubs with their mommies.
Cupcake is so happy she can hardly believe that she is on her first safari.

Cupcake rides in a jeep with no real doors or windows,
staring in wonder at the hippos and buffaloes.
Giraffes walk with each other like they are going to school.
Their long spotted-brown legs make them look cool.
Every animal in Cupcake's picture books is here.
Some run far away from her, and others come near..

The next day, Mom and Dad want to learn about Kenya's history.
So everyone goes to the National Museum in Nairobi, a place full of mystery.
There are long hallways that make the girls want to race.
"No, no," says Mommy, for this is not the place.

Cupcake sees pictures on the wall but does not know what they
mean. There are pictures of kids and even a queen.
Leaving the museum, Cupcake races past the door.
She wants to take a picture with the giant dinosaur!

On the third day, Cupcake and Noodles rise early for their adventure.
The whole family is going to the Giraffe Centre.
Giraffes, giraffes are everywhere-long necks here and long necks there.
Noodles feeds the happy giraffe a pellet.
His sticky tongue is long and his breath, whew! Even Noodles can smell it.

Giraffes walk all around and Noodles reaches for a giraffe's mouth.
She wants to pet her, no doubt.
Noodles has no more pellets, so it is time to go.
But a giraffe still sticks out her tongue for food because she doesn't know.
The pellets are all gone, we are sad to say. Noodles will have to come back another day.

On this fourth day, Cupcake and Noodles may wonder what they will see
as they visit the elephant sanctuary.
November is cool, and the rains make mud.
The orphaned baby elephants playing in the wet dirt looks fun.
The elephants walk in mud so red. They put mud on their backs, legs and heads.

The elephant is the largest land mammal in the world;
Cupcake reaches to touch one of the big girls.
This elephant will grow big and strong, with her tusks up high and trunk hanging long.
Cupcake knows she has made a new friend; and it looks like the elephant walked off with a grin.

Then snap! Whoaaa!!!! An elephant starts to run! He bumps into the ropes with all his tons.
It scares Cupcake, and she grabs her dad. He picks her up in his arms, which makes her glad.
"See ya later, elephants!" Cupcake yells. Those big red elephants are really swell.

The last full day brings a plane ride to the city of Mombasa to play on the beach in the sun.
Cupcake and Noodles put on bathing suits to start the fun.
They play near the water slide before Noodles joins Mommy for a beach camel ride.
Later, Noodles lies in the hammock and tries to swing.
Oops! She almost falls out; it is a very funny thing.

The hotel has lots of food-all you-can-eat cookies, carrots, and all kinds of treats.
A huge screen is set up on the grass for watching a movie.
Cartoons near the beach-how groovy!
Noodles finds a seat in the sand and lets the dirt run through her hands.
Cupcake and Noodles want to stay, but they must go back home without delay.

Bye-bye, Kenya....
Mom and Dad will take them another place, since they all like to roam.
But now it's time to go back home.
Cupcake and Noodles are on the plane in their blankets all curled,
thinking about their next adventure somewhere in the world!

Want to know more about the places
Cupcake and Noodles visited in Kenya?

Nairobi National Park: http://www.museums.or.ke/
Nairobi National Museum: http://www.museums.or.ke/
Giraffe Centre: https://giraffecenter.org/
David Sheldrick's Elephant Orphanage: https://www.sheldrickwildlifetrust.org/
Mombasa: http://www.magicalkenya.com/places-to-visit/cities/mombasa/
Five Reasons to visit Nairobi, Kenya: http://raisingnomads.com/3509-2/

about the series

Cupcake and Noodles Go To... is a children's book series for kids aged preschool to second grade. The books are the real-life adventures of two American sisters, Cupcake and Noodles (their nicknames), as they travel the world with their mom and dad and learn about other cultures. Sometimes, other family members tag along! When the girls traveled to Kenya, Cupcake was two years old, and Noodles was one.

Come along and grow with Cupcake and Noodles as they learn and share about the world. These are the lived experiences of the girls. The places you read about are the actual places they visited with their parents. The illustrations in the book series are animated versions of actual photos taken by Cupcake and Noodles's parents on their trips! Some of the text reflects the actual words or expressions of the girls.

Have fun learning about the beautiful places in the world through the eyes of children who have experienced it. For moms and dads, there is a handy guide at the back of each book with the websites of each of the places visited in case you want to take your family on this same adventure. Stay tuned for upcoming books on New Zealand; Spain; Washington, DC; Chile; and New York. Let's roam the world together!

about the author

A native of Houston, Texas, Angie Stubbs conceived the Cupcake and Noodles series to highlight the adventures she has with her family as they roam the world together. She is an attorney by training and graduated from Xavier University of Louisiana and the George Washington University School of Law. Along with her husband and their two preschoolers, she is an avid traveler who hopes to inspire families to explore the world. Angie enjoys cooking, reading and exercising in her spare time.

CPSIA information can be obtained
at www.ICGtesting.com
Printed in the USA
BVHW02s1328020818
523207BV00009B/13/P